Alice Walker

•••

There Is a Flower at the Tip of My Nose Smelling Me

Illustrations by

Stefano Vitale

HarperCollins Publishers

There is a flower
At the tip
Of my nose
Smelling
Me.

There is a sky
At the end
Of my
Eye
Seeing
Me.

There is a road
At the bottom
Of my
Foot
Walking me.

There is a dog
At the end
Of my leash
Holding
Me.

There is an ocean
At the top
Of my
Head
Swimming me.

There is a sunrise
At the edge
Of
My skin
Praising
Me.

There is water
At the tip
Of my tongue
Tasting me.

There is a song
Deep in
My body
Singing
Me.

There is a dance
That lives
In my bones
Dancing
Me.

There is a poem
In the cradle
Of my Soul
Rocking me.

There is a pen
Nestled
In my hand
Writing
Me.

There is a story
At the end
Of my arms
Telling
Me!

A Note from the Author

One day I went walking in the forest near my house with my dog, along an old logging trail. Redwoods rose to left and right, the sky was brilliant blue with a few threads of clouds, the earth was scented with spring. As I walked, the wonder of myself as part of all this overcame me. I began to sing: "I come out of You, my Love. I come out of You!" Over and over, with the greatest gratitude and joy. As soon as I got home, my big black lab trotting just as happily beside me, I wrote this book, which was not a book then, but a thank you note.

• • •

There Is a Flower at the Tip of My Nose Smelling Me

Text copyright © 2006 by Alice Walker

Illustrations copyright © 2006 by Stefano Vitale

Manufactured in China.

All rights reserved.

www.harperchildrens.com

Library of Congress Cataloging-in-Publication Data

Walker, Alice, date.

There is a flower at the tip of my nose smelling me / by Alice Walker; illustrated by Stefano Vitale. — 1st ed.

p.   cm.

ISBN-10: 0-06-057080-6 (trade bdg.) — ISBN-13: 978-0-06-057080-4 (trade bdg.)

ISBN-10: 0-06-057081-4 (lib. bdg.) — ISBN-13: 978-0-06-057081-1 (lib. bdg.)

1. Self—Juvenile poetry. 2. Children's poetry, American. I. Vitale, Stefano.

II. Title.

PS3573.A425T467 2006

811'.54—dc22   2005014617

Design by Martha Rago

1 2 3 4 5 6 7 8 9 10 ❖ First Edition